D0506748

Cat Claws to Thumbtacks

Tech from Nature

By Jennifer Colby

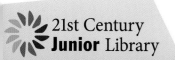

21st Century
Junior Library

Published in the United States of America by
Cherry Lake Publishing
Ann Arbor, Michigan
www.cherrylakepublishing.com

Reading Adviser: Marla Conn, MS, Ed., Literacy specialist, Read-Ability, Inc.
Content Adviser: Rachel Brown, MA, Sustainable Business

Photo Credits: © ihorga/Shutterstock.com, Cover, 1 [left]; ©Anna_Huchak/Shutterstock.com, Cover, 1 [right];
© Mirror-Images/Shutterstock.com, 4; © bousole/Flickr, 6; © Naomi Sweet/Shutterstock.com, 8; © Edwin Moore
(US654319A)/United States Patent and Trademark Office, 10; © Internet Archive Book/Flickr, 12; © dangdumrong/
Shutterstock.com, 14; © Seregraff/Shutterstock.com, 16; © Toshi Fukaya, 18, 20

Library of Congress Cataloging-in-Publication Data

Names: Colby, Jennifer, author.
Title: Cat claws to thumbtacks / Jennifer Colby.
Description: Ann Arbor : Cherry Lake Publishing, [2019] | Includes bibliographical references and index. |
    Audience: Grades 4 to 6.
Identifiers: LCCN 2018035554 | ISBN 9781534142954 (hardcover) | ISBN 9781534140714 (pdf) |
    ISBN 9781534139510 (pbk.) | ISBN 9781534141919 (hosted ebook)
Subjects: LCSH: Tacks—Juvenile literature. | Claws—Juvenile literature. | Biomimicry—Juvenile literature.
Classification: LCC TS440 C65 2019 | DDC 600—dc23
LC record available at https://lccn.loc.gov/2018035554

Cherry Lake Publishing would like to acknowledge the work of the Partnership for 21st Century Skills.
Please visit *www.p21.org* for more information.

Printed in the United States of America
Corporate Graphics

CONTENTS

Do you have thumbtacks at home?

Everyday Item

You have probably seen a thumbtack. They are mainly used to hold up pieces of paper on walls. But people use them for other things, too.

Thumbtacks and pushpins can also be used in art projects!

Useful Things

Thumbtacks are used in schools, offices, and homes all over the world. You probably see them every day. Thumbtacks, pushpins, and map pins are all similar. These pins have a sharp end. The end is meant to **pierce** through an item, like a piece of paper. It attaches that item to something, such as a wall.

They have many purposes. People use pushpins on a map to track where they've been. Furniture makers use thumbtacks to **upholster** chairs and couches. Thumbtacks

Be careful not to leave a thumbtack on the floor!

can be used to decorate an object. You might have used thumbtacks or pushpins to hang photos on a wall or bulletin board.

The design of thumbtacks has not changed much over the years. They are simple. There is little need for improvement. But have you ever stepped on one? Ouch! The study of cat claws has made thumbtacks safer. How is this possible? Let's take a closer look at the history of thumbtacks and how they've been improved.

Look!

Search around your home. What does your family use thumbtacks for? Look around your classroom. What does your teacher use thumbtacks for?

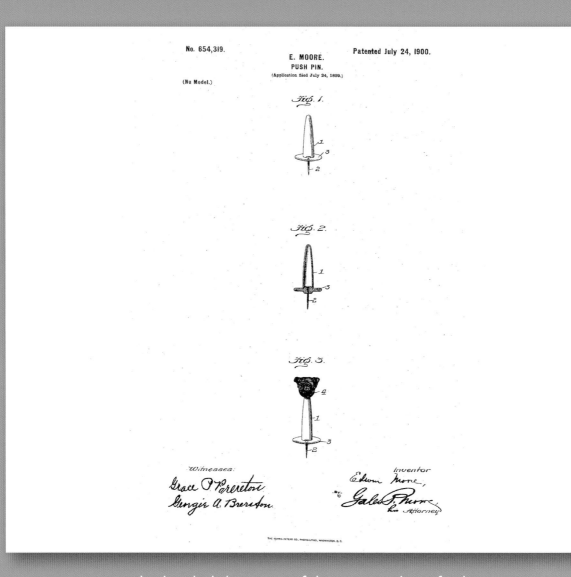

Moore made detailed drawings of the new pushpin for his patent.

Patent to Production

The pushpin was first **patented** in 1900 by Edwin Moore. He had an idea for a new kind of pushpin. Before, people used drawing pins. These had flat heads that were usually made of wood and metal. Unlike the drawing pin, Moore's pin would not **corrode** when **exposed** to water. His pushpin was made out of glass and steel. It also had a "handle." This made it easier to push in and pull out.

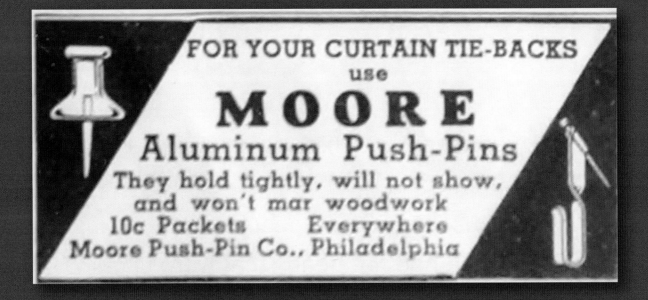

An early advertisement.

In his patent application, Moore explained that it was cheap and easy to make. He also explained that the pushpin was always ready to be used. He started producing them right away.

Moore worked hard every day to make pushpins. Soon he was filling large orders for big companies.

Over the years, Moore patented other items, including map tacks and picture hangers. His company was dedicated to making **devices** for hanging up little things.

How could these be improved?

Thumbtacks and pushpins are simple devices. But a new design has made them much safer.

In 2011, a New York designer named Toshi Fukaya designed a **retractable** thumbtack. He was **inspired** by the claws of his cat.

Think!

What is special about cat claws? How would they inspire a new kind of thumbtack? Share your thoughts with a friend.

Cat's claws are retractable.

Investigating Nature

Do you have a cat? Does your cat have claws? You would know if it does. A cat's claws are sharp! Unlike some animals, cats can retract their claws. That means they can expose them only when they need to.

Cats and other **felines** expose their claws when they hunt or when they need to protect themselves. Cats also expose their claws when they're stretching! Most of the time,

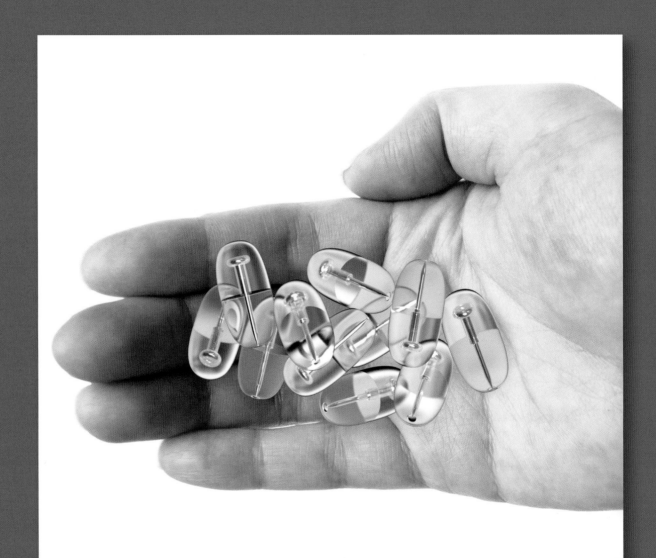

Fukaya's thumbtacks are safer to use.

cats do not need their claws. By retracting them, a cat can keep its claws sharp.

Fukaya's design is simple. When not in use, the sharp point of the pushpin is covered. A **silicone** cap covers the pin. It protects the user. You can pick them up or step on them, and you will not be hurt.

When pushed into a board, the hard handle of the device pushes the pin through the soft silicone cap. This makes it much safer than a regular pushpin.

Make a Guess!

What other animals have retractable claws? Make a list, and then ask an adult to help you find the answers.

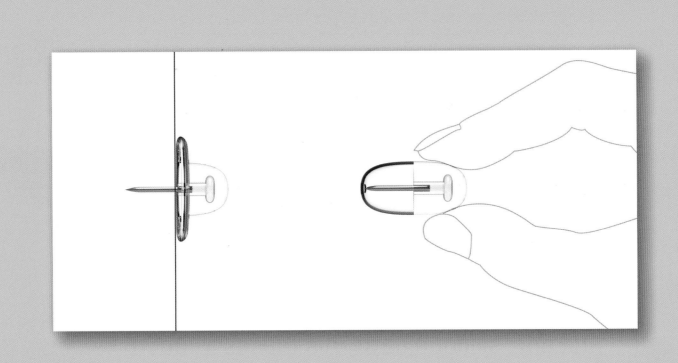

The pin is only exposed when pushed into a board.

Fukaya studied the special **anatomy** of a cat's paw. His invention was based on the concept of **biomimicry**. Biomimicry is a rapidly growing scientific field of research.

You can thank Fukaya and cats for making thumbtacks safer to use!

Ask Questions!

Are you interested in inventing something new? Find out what it takes to get a patent. Ask a librarian to help you. Then, look to nature for inspiration!

GLOSSARY

anatomy (uh-NAT-uh-mee) the parts that form a living thing

biomimicry (bye-oh-MIM-ik-ree) copying plants and animals to build or improve something

corrode (kuh-ROHD) to gradually destroy or weaken

devices (dih-VISE-iz) pieces of equipment that do particular jobs

exposed (ik-SPOHZD) showed or revealed

felines (FEE-linez) members of the cat family

inspired (in-SPYRD) having had an idea about what to create based on something else

patented (PAT-uhnt-id) given the legal right to be made and sold by a specific person or company, for a certain period of time

pierce (PEERS) to make a hole in or through something

retractable (rih-TRAKT-uh-buhl) something that can be pulled back into something that covers it

silicone (SIL-ih-kohn) a type of material that does not let water or heat pass through; often used to make rubber and grease

upholster (uhp-HOHL-ster) to put a covering of material on a piece of furniture

FIND OUT MORE

BOOKS

The Everything Book of Cats and Kittens. New York: DK Children, 2018.

Inventions: A Visual Encyclopedia. New York: DK Children, 2018.

WEBSITES

Inventive Kids
http://inventivekids.com
Learn about inventions and inventors, inventions, and how you can become an inventor.

Paws—About Cats
www.paws.org/kids/learn/pets/cats
Learn more about cats and how to care for them.

INDEX

ABOUT THE AUTHOR

Jennifer Colby is a school librarian in Ann Arbor, Michigan. She loves reading, traveling, and going to museums to learn about new things.